Countries Around the World

South Africa

Claire Throp

Heinemann Library
Chicago, Illinois

www.capstonepub.com
Visit our website to find out more information about Heinemann-Raintree books.

To order:
☎ Phone 888-454-2279
💻 Visit www.capstonepub.com
to browse our catalog and order online.

Edited by Catherine Veitch and Charlotte Guillain
Designed by Steve Mead
Original illustrations © Capstone Global Library Ltd 2012
Illustrated by Oxford Designers & Illustrators
Picture research by Hannah Taylor
Originated by Capstone Global Library Ltd
Printed in China by CTPS

15 14 13 12 11
10 9 8 7 6 5 4 3 2 1

Library of Congress Cataloging-in-Publication Data
Throp, Claire.
  South Africa / Claire Throp.
    p. cm.—(Countries around the world)
  Includes bibliographical references and index.
  ISBN 978-1-4329-6112-1 (hb)—ISBN 978-1-4329-6138-1 (pb) 1. South Africa—Juvenile literature. 2. South Africa—History—Juvenile literature. I. Title.
  DT1719.T57 2012
  968—dc22   2011015806

Acknowledgments
We would like to thank the following for permission to reproduce photographs: Corbis pp. 9 (Bettmann), 12 (Peter Turnley), 21 (Frans Lanting), 34 (Reuters/Mike Hutchings), 35 (Eva-Lotta Jansson); Dreamstime pp. 7 (© Nico Smit), 15 (© Kaz2), 29 (© Anke Van Wyk), 30 (© Temistocle Lucarelli); Getty Images pp. 8 (Hulton Archive), 10, 11, 23, 31 (AFP), 26 (Stuart Fox), 37 (Per-Anders Pettersson); Photolibrary pp. 27 (Imagebroker.net/ Ulrich Doering), 33 (Radius Images); Shutterstock pp. 5 (© fotum), 17 (© Daleen Loest), 18 (© WA van den Noort), 19 (© Four Oaks), 25 (© Socrates), 39 (© Neil Bradfield).

Cover photograph of a leopard in a nature reserve in South Africa reproduced with permission of Dreamstime.com (© Hedrus).

Every effort has been made to contact copyright holders of material reproduced in this book. Any omissions will be rectified in subsequent printings if notice is given to the publisher.

The publishers would like to thank Dr. Damian Walter for his assistance in the preparation of this book.

Contents

Some words in the book are in bold, **like this**. You can find out what they mean by looking in the glossary.

Introducing South Africa

What comes to mind when you think of South Africa? Amazing African animals, such as elephants or lions? Nelson Mandela? Or perhaps diamonds and gold? South Africa is famous for all these things and more. Its difficult political history, in particular the years of **apartheid**, has cast a shadow over what is one of the most interesting countries in the world.

South Africa lies at the bottom of Africa. It is over seven times the size of California. The Prince Edward Islands in the southern Indian Ocean also belong to the country. South Africa shares a border with Botswana, Namibia, Zimbabwe, Mozambique, Lesotho, and Swaziland. The Atlantic Ocean and the Indian Ocean meet at the southernmost tip of the country.

People have lived in South Africa for thousands of years. **Fossils** of the earliest humans have been found there. It has the biggest **economy** in Africa, and its people come from a range of backgrounds. This is shown by the fact that the country has 11 official languages!

Variety and tradition

South Africa is a great attraction for tourists who want to experience the variety of geographical landscapes and learn more about the traditional African way of life. However, it is also a country that is still trying to improve the lives of the many South Africans who suffered during apartheid.

How to say...

English	Afrikaans		Zulu	
Hi	*Haai*	(hi)	*Sawubona*	(sa-woo-bo-na)
How are you?	*Hoe gaan dit?*	(hoo-gaan-dit)	*Unjani?*	(un-jah-nee)
Goodbye	*Totsiens*	(tot-seens)	*Sala kahle*	(sah-la kah-leh)

The giraffe is one of the many amazing animals that can be seen in South Africa.

History: Overcoming Difficulties

Scientists agree that the earliest modern humans existed in South Africa 100,000 to 200,000 years ago. Early communities that lived in South Africa included the San, who were **hunter-gatherers**, and the Khoikhoi, who were animal herders. From about the 3rd century CE, they began to trade with people who brought new ideas about agriculture.

The Europeans arrive

In the mid-1600s, the Dutch East India Company set up what is now Cape Town and traded with the Khoikhoi. By the 1700s, the Dutch descendants—called trekboers or **Boers** (later called Afrikaners)—were independent farmers. Gradually, the Africans lost their lands and were forced to become servants.

After the British took over the Cape area in 1806, the Boers moved farther north, as part of what became known as the Great Trek. They eventually set up two **republics**, called the Transvaal and the Orange Free State.

SHAKA KASENZANGAKHONA
(ABOUT 1787–1828)

Shaka kaSenzangakhona was a Zulu leader. He brought many neighboring groups into his Zulu kingdom through conquest and **assimilation**. Shaka came to power by staging a takeover after the death of his father. He was eventually killed by his half-brother. In 1830 the Zulu nation formed the most powerful independent African kingdom in southern Africa.

San rock art is the earliest known form of art in South Africa.

Diamonds and gold

The discovery of diamonds in 1867 and gold in 1886 changed South Africa's **economy** hugely. This once-agricultural country changed to one based on industry and trade. At first, people flocked to South Africa to make their fortunes from the diamond and gold mines. Eventually, all the mines were bought up by large companies.

Anglo-Zulu War, 1879

In 1879 British and **colonial** soldiers invaded Zululand. A British force was beaten by the Zulus at Isandhlwana. This was an incredible defeat, as the well-armed British forces were defeated by an army that fought only with spears and shields. However, the British eventually conquered Zululand in 1887 with their superior weapons.

The Boer Wars

The British and the **Boers** fought wars over the lands containing diamond and gold mines. The British were at a disadvantage, because they did not know the land as well as the Boers. They used what was called a scorched-earth policy. This involved burning farms and sending African workers, as well as Boer women and children, to **concentration camps**. Poor organization meant that food and medicine often ran out, and many of the imprisoned people died.

British soldiers fought in trenches in the second Boer War (1899–1902).

Union of South Africa

In 1910 the British and Boer states joined together to become the Union of South Africa. Very few black South Africans or people with **mixed ancestry** were able to vote in elections, and none was allowed to run for **parliament**. White women did not receive the vote until 1930. The organization that later became the African National Congress (ANC) was formed in 1912, to try to change the situation for black South Africans and those of mixed ancestry.

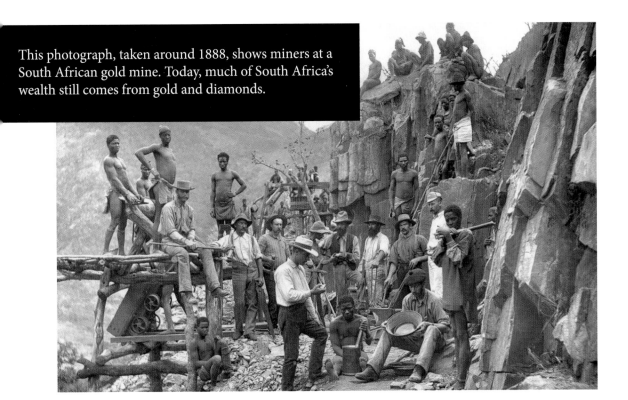

This photograph, taken around 1888, shows miners at a South African gold mine. Today, much of South Africa's wealth still comes from gold and diamonds.

How to say...

English	Afrikaans	Zulu
diamond	*diamante* (dee-a-mon-ta)	*idayimani* (ee-day-ee-mahni)
gold	*goud* (howt)	*igolide* (ee-go-lee-de)
silver	*silwer* (sil-ver)	*isiliver* (ee-see-lee-va)

Apartheid

Apartheid was the system used by the Afrikaner National Party to keep black and white people separate. Although apartheid was not made law until 1950, the system was in place well before that. In 1913, for example, white South Africans were given 87 percent of the land. Black South Africans had to go to different schools, use different buses, and live in separate areas. In 1952 Pass Laws forced non-white people to carry identity papers at all times or risk arrest. This greatly restricted their freedom.

1960s

At a peaceful protest against the Pass Laws at Sharpeville in 1960, police killed 69 people and injured over 180. As a result, the government banned public meetings. They also later banned the ANC. In 1964 the ANC leader Nelson Mandela was put in prison for life.

WINNIE MANDELA

(BORN 1936)

Winnie Mandela was known as "Mother of the Nation" because of her support for her imprisoned husband, Nelson, and her work against apartheid. However, in the 1980s Winnie's reputation was ruined by her connection to violence and her possible link to the death of a teenager, Stompie Moeketsi. Shortly after Nelson was released from prison, he and Winnie divorced.

Increasing violence

The Soweto Uprising of 1976 took place when students protested against having their classes taught in Afrikaans. The protest began peacefully, but police fired into the crowd. The situation turned into a full-scale riot, and over the following year hundreds were killed. One of these was Steve Biko, a black leader who was killed while in police **custody**.

Afrikaans was the language associated with white people and the government responsible for apartheid. Black South Africans wanted to be taught in their own languages.

International disapproval

In 1986 **economic sanctions** against South Africa were put in place by many countries, including the United States. This meant that South Africa could not earn money by selling goods to other countries. People across the world disliked the way the South African government treated the majority of its people. A new president, F. W. de Klerk, realized that things had to change.

Change at last

Finally, after 27 years in prison, Nelson Mandela was released in 1990. His release was followed by **democratic** elections in 1994 and the ending of apartheid. The ANC won, and Mandela became the new president. In 1995 the Truth and Reconciliation Commission was set up to investigate violence during the apartheid years.

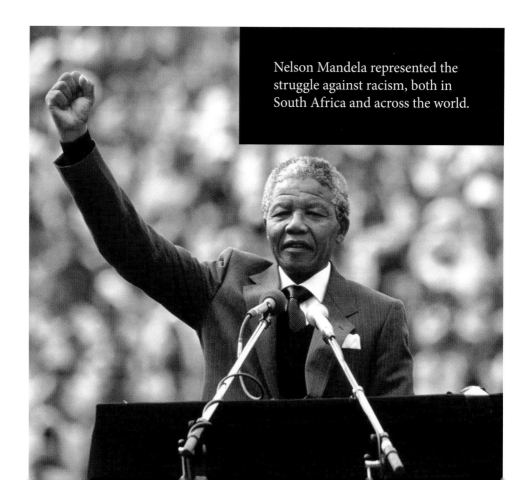

Nelson Mandela represented the struggle against racism, both in South Africa and across the world.

Daily life

In the years since apartheid ended, new houses have been built for the poor, many of whom now have electricity and access to water. A black middle class has emerged, and more foreign **investment** has improved the economy. However, crime is still high, as is unemployment. Millions of people have HIV/AIDS, and there is still a huge gap between the rich and poor.

Moving forward

Today, the ANC is still in power, under the leadership of President Jacob Zuma. The National Party no longer exists. South Africa is dealing with issues such as **HIV/AIDS** and the **recession** that followed the global financial crisis in 2008. However, major sports events recently held in South Africa have helped to unite the country, if only for a short time.

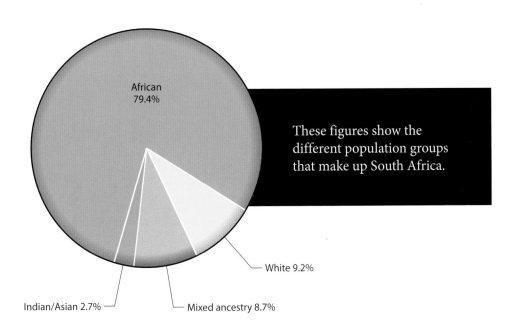

African 79.4%

These figures show the different population groups that make up South Africa.

White 9.2%

Mixed ancestry 8.7%

Indian/Asian 2.7%

Regions and Resources: All That Glitters

South Africa has a wide range of different landscapes, from high mountains and grasslands to desert and coastal plains. South Africa has nine provinces. Northern Cape has the fewest people, due to its desert landscape. Eastern Cape is quiet with relatively few tourists, while KwaZulu-Natal is famous for its beaches.

Climate

When it is winter in North America and Europe, it is summer in South Africa. This is because South Africa is in the half of the world called the southern hemisphere. The climate is generally warm and sunny, but higher land is usually cooler. The eastern coast has subtropical temperatures with hot, humid summers. Rainfall is generally low, which can lead to water shortages. The east and south are the wettest.

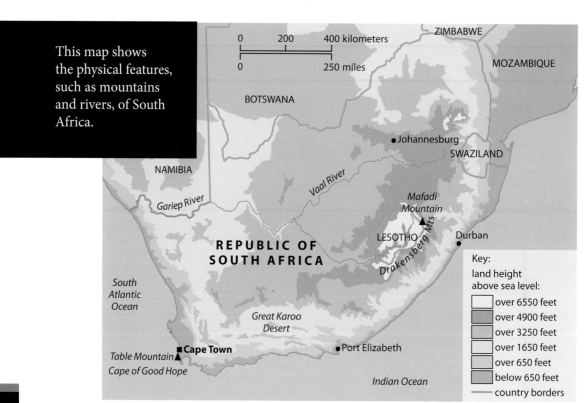

This map shows the physical features, such as mountains and rivers, of South Africa.

Rivers, mountains, and a volcano

There are very few rivers in South Africa because of the climate. The Gariep River (also known as the Orange River) is the longest, at 1,300 miles (2,092 kilometers). It begins in the Drakensberg Mountains and travels westward across the country.

The Drakensberg Mountains are in eastern South Africa. Mafadi is the highest point in South Africa, at 11,319 feet (3,450 meters). Table Mountain, overlooking Cape Town, is well known for its flat top.

South Africa's only volcano is the one that formed Marion Island, part of the Prince Edward Islands. It last erupted in 2004. The Prince Edward Islands are located about 1,118 miles (1,800 kilometers) southeast of Port Elizabeth.

Drakensberg Mountains means "Dragon Mountains" in Afrikaans. Zulus call it uKhahlamba, which means "barrier of spears."

Resources

Much of South Africa's wealth comes from minerals. In addition to diamonds and gold, the country is one of the world's top producers of platinum.

Trade

South Africa's trading partners include the United States, the United Kingdom, Japan, and Germany. The main **exports** are diamonds, gold, platinum, and machinery. South Africa was the fourth-largest exporter of coal in 2005. **Imports** include machinery and equipment, as well as some foods.

Jobs and industry

Fishing is an important industry, particularly on the west coast. Food crops include pineapples, maize (corn), and sugarcane. Grapes are also grown for winemaking. Key industries include the manufacture of goods such as vehicles, textiles (cloths), and electronic equipment. Tourism is a major source of income, although high crime rates can make some tourists not want to visit the country. Around one million people are employed in the tourism industry, working in restaurants, hotels, and as guides.

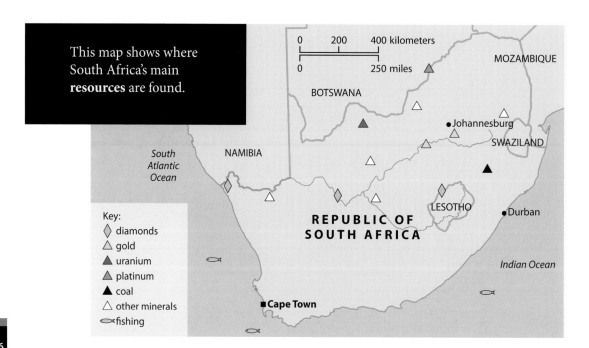

This map shows where South Africa's main **resources** are found.

The Big Hole in Kimberley is the site of a diamond mine. It is the largest human-made hole on Earth.

Daily life

White people still have many of the best jobs in South Africa. The policy of Black Economic Empowerment (BEE), brought in by the ANC when they came to power, aimed to redistribute wealth and ownership to disadvantaged people. This involved ideas such as companies offering shares to their black employees. Share ownership means the person owns part of the company, even if it is only a small part. However, most people now agree that the BEE policy has failed. Even the current president, Jacob Zuma, agrees that instead of redistributing wealth, the policy has simply led to "a few individuals benefitting a lot." In 2010 the president promised a review of the policy.

Wildlife: The Biggest and the Smallest

South Africa covers about 2 percent of the world's land area, but it has about 10 percent of the plant **species** and 7 percent of the world's reptiles, mammals, and birds.

National parks

There are 20 national parks in South Africa. They have had success with the **conservation** of rare species. Numbers of white rhinos in Kruger National Park more than doubled from 1989 to 1995. Mountain Zebra National Park was set up in 1937 with the aim of saving the Cape mountain zebra, which was near **extinction**. There are now 300 zebras in the park.

South Africa is famous for the "Big Five" animals: elephants, lions, leopards, rhinoceroses, and buffalos. The term "Big Five" refers to the fact that they were once thought to be the five most dangerous animals to hunt and kill. Today, these animals are protected, and the chance to see them on safari proves to be a major attraction for tourists.

Elephants are one of the "Big Five" animals that people visit South Africa to see.

Whales and penguins

Whale Coast, near Cape Town, is great for land-based whale watching. Southern right whales visit between June and November and can be seen with their calves all along the coast. Penguins have also established two colonies on the mainland near Cape Town. In 2000, African penguins were rescued by a huge international conservation effort after an oil leak threatened their breeding ground on Dassen Island, near Cape Town.

African penguins are known for making a strange noise that sounds like a donkey.

How to say...

English	Afrikaans		Zulu	
elephant	*olifant*	(o-lee-fant)	*indlovu*	(in-glo-voo)
rhinoceros	*renoster*	(re-nos-ter)	*ubhejane*	(oo-beh-ja-ne)
giraffe	*kameelperd*	(ka-meel-perd)	*indlulamithi*	(in-glu-la-mee-tee)

Cape Floral Kingdom

South Africa has its own **ecosystem**, Cape Floral Kingdom. Its eight protected areas cover less than 0.5 percent of Africa, but they contain 20 percent of all the plant species on the continent. It is the only one of the world's six floral kingdoms to be found within a single country.

Environmental issues

The world's biggest **solar** power plant is being built in Northern Cape to produce a tenth of the country's power. The government had been criticized for plans to build a coal-fired power plant. The country gets over 90 percent of its power from burning coal. Solar power is **renewable energy**, while coal is not, so solar power is much less damaging to the environment.

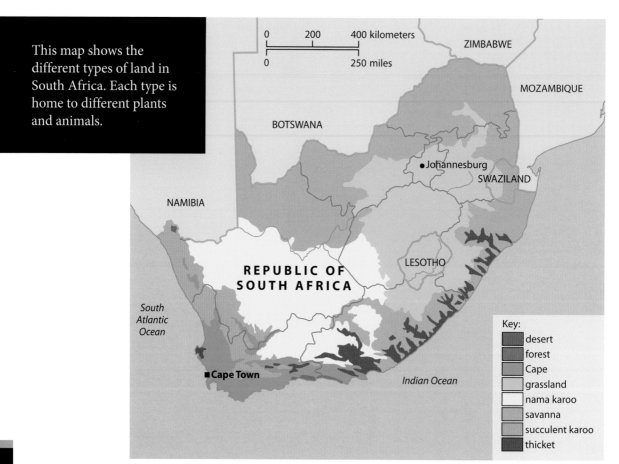

This map shows the different types of land in South Africa. Each type is home to different plants and animals.

Key:
- desert
- forest
- Cape
- grassland
- nama karoo
- savanna
- succulent karoo
- thicket

Namaqualand is a semi-desert area. But when it rains in the spring, millions of wildflowers come into bloom.

Many rivers and **wetlands** in South Africa are polluted with agricultural fertilizers. Mining has also caused problems. Streams near Johannesburg were found to contain poisons such as cyanide and arsenic. In areas near cities, factories and car exhausts cause air pollution.

Water

Water conservation is extremely important in South Africa, as water shortages are common. The west of the country is particularly affected. Not only is there not enough water, but the water quality is also often not very good. South Africa has over 500 dams. The largest is Gariep Dam on the Gariep River, built as part of the Orange River Project in the early 1970s. The project allowed water to be redirected and used for irrigation. It is used to produce **hydroelectric power** and to provide water for homes and industry.

Infrastructure: Democracy and Freedom

South Africa has a **democratically** elected government. This means people vote for the South Africans they want to run the country. Everyone over 18 has the right to vote.

Parliament and local government

South Africa is led by a president and two houses of **parliament**. The president can rule for two five-year terms at the most. The National Council of Provinces has 90 members. The National Assembly has 350 to 400 members, who are elected for five years. Each of the provinces also has its own local government. Most countries have one capital city, but South Africa has three: Pretoria, Cape Town (where parliament meets), and Bloemfontein (where the law courts are based).

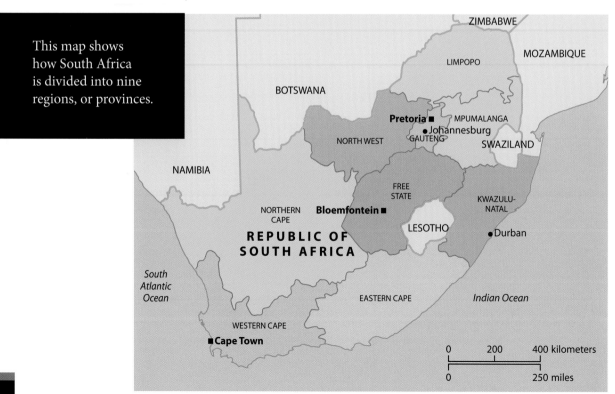

This map shows how South Africa is divided into nine regions, or provinces.

Media

Since 1994 people who work in the South African media, such as newspaper reporters, have had a lot more freedom. An organization called Reporters Without Borders investigates press freedom around the world every year. In 2010 they ranked South Africa 38th out of 178 countries.

The South African Broadcasting Company is the state-run main broadcaster. Many commercial television and radio stations reflect the different cultures in South Africa.

YOUNG PEOPLE

In 2009 the Junior 8 summit took place in Rome, Italy. Teenagers from many countries, including South Africa, took part in discussions about the global financial crisis, climate change, and poverty. Four South Africans, between the ages of 14 and 17, represented their country. None of them had left South Africa before. The summit gave them an opportunity to discuss important subjects with the **G8** leaders who were meeting at the same time.

Black South Africans were finally able to vote in the election of 1994. The ANC won the election.

Technology

Only about 10 percent of the South African population was using the Internet by 2009. This is partly because it is expensive to access. As in many other countries, it is also harder to get access in poorer **rural** areas. Cell phone use is increasing, with 45 million cell phones in use in 2008.

Daily life

HIV/AIDS is a big problem in South Africa, with 5.7 million people HIV positive. Almost 280,000 children under the age of 15 are HIV positive. It is thought that only 37 percent of infected people were receiving treatment at the end of 2009. The government has been criticized because it was too slow to react to the crisis. This lack of action allowed the disease to spread quickly.

This graph shows the **life expectancy** in South Africa, in comparison with the United States and the United Kingdom. The life expectancy rate in South Africa fell in the 1990s partly due to the HIV/AIDS crisis.

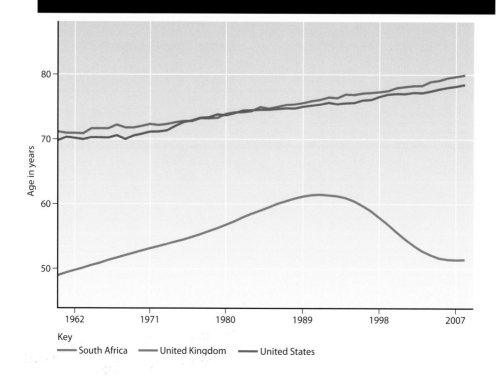

Key
— South Africa   — United Kingdom   — United States

Housing

Houses in South Africa range from the large mansions of the rich to the mud huts or metal shacks of the poor. Housing shortages are a problem. **Townships** are towns on the edge of a city that were home to non-white South Africans during the **apartheid** years. Townships still exist, but some of the poorest homes have been improved, with basic brick houses becoming more common. It is thought that about 83 percent now have electricity. Unfortunately, power outages are still common.

The gap between rich and poor is still large. Many homes in the townships have improved in recent years, however.

School

South African children between the ages of seven and fifteen must go to school. Children under seven go to nursery school. They spend the next seven years at elementary school. Children then go to high school for at least two years, but they can stay on for another three years. College is open to anyone who gets the right grades in at least three subjects.

School is only free for the poorest families. Others need to pay fees, and parents also have to pay for textbooks. The government is continuing to make more schooling free, however.

South African schoolchildren wear school uniforms. In some schools, there is one day a week when the children can wear their normal clothes.

School hours are usually 7:50 a.m. until 2:30 p.m. Some children in South Africa have to travel long distances to get to school. The school year begins in January. Winter vacation lasts about two months, from late July. Summer vacation is from early December to late January.

Classes

Classes include math, history, science, and art. Some rural schools do not have up-to-date equipment such as computers, but this is gradually changing. Classes can be given in any of the 11 official languages, but English is usually taught as well. Schoolchildren play sports such as soccer, **cricket**, netball (which is similar to basketball), and volleyball.

YOUNG PEOPLE

Lots of children enjoy playing soccer, going swimming, or skipping in their free time. Sometimes they make up games with things they find, such as old tires. In Zulu culture, girls sometimes become majorettes who accompany bands. The majorettes have to learn how to twirl a baton.

These boys are enjoying a game of soccer, one of the most popular sports in South Africa.

Culture: Sports, Music, and Braaie

Different areas of the country are home to different black South African **ethnic** groups, each with its own language and cultural background, including Zulus, Xhosa, Ndebele, Swazi, and Sotho. Many still live in areas that they were forced into during the **apartheid** period. Some traditional settlements remain, but many people now live in average suburbs. They try to keep some traditions going, however, such as traditional dancing, **faith healing**, and beadwork.

Daily life

South Africa has many laws to protect women's rights. Women hold 44 percent of seats in **parliament**, and Helen Zille is the leader of a major political party. However, in business there are very few women in top roles. In traditional black households, men are in charge. In some **rural** areas, women walk several paces behind men, and violence toward women is more common than elsewhere in the country. In general, some women's lives may be improving, but there is still much work to be done.

Music and dance

A mix of traditional African and Western styles can be seen in South African music and dance. Kwaito is rap music that is based on protest chants and American and British dance music. Gospel choirs are a traditional form of entertainment, and jazz is also enjoyed throughout South Africa. Many South African dance companies perform around the world. Traditional African dancing is linked to occasions such as weddings.

Zulu dancers sometimes perform traditional African dances for tourists.

Literature and art

For most of the 1900s, authors were not allowed to write about apartheid. If they challenged the government, their books were banned. Now there is more freedom for people to write about the country. South Africa's best-known authors include J. M. Coetzee and Nadine Gordimer.

Some of the most beautiful South African art includes Zulu beadwork. Different colored beads mean different things, so when they are put together in a certain pattern they can form a message. These messages can include love letters or even an offer of marriage!

Religion

In traditional African religions, faith healers use local medicines to heal body and mind. There is a strong tradition of **ancestor** worship, as well as a belief in spirits that inhabit the natural world, including rocks and plants.

This woman is a sangoma. A sangoma is a Zulu healer or herbalist.

Most South Africans are Christian, and there are over 4,000 independent churches in the country. The Zion Christian Church, for example, combines Christianity with more traditional African beliefs. Islam was introduced to South Africa by Malay slaves brought from Dutch colonies in Southeast Asia. Hinduism arrived with workers brought to South Africa from the Indian subcontinent.

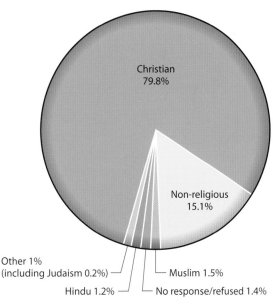

Christian
79.8%

Non-religious
15.1%

Other 1%
(including Judaism 0.2%)

Muslim 1.5%

Hindu 1.2%

No response/refused 1.4%

This chart shows the religions practiced in South Africa.

Festivals and national holidays

Festivals are celebrated throughout the year in South Africa. The Prickly Pear Festival is held in late February or early March in Nelson Mandela Bay. It is a day when everyone celebrates traditional South African food. The famous National Arts Festival takes place in Grahamstown in June, and the Hermanus Whale Festival is in September. In 2010, 130,000 people turned up to see the whales in their natural setting!

Food

The different backgrounds of South African people are shown in the number of different cooking styles found around the country. Sweet, spicy curries are common in Cape Malay, and a popular European dish is a stew called *potjiekos*, cooked in a traditional three-legged pot. In KwaZulu-Natal you can eat bunny chow, an Indian-style curry served in a hollowed-out loaf of bread. Tripe is popular particularly with black South Africans. Tripe is made from the stomach tissues of cows, sheep, and other animals.

The staple food for poorer families is pap, which is a type of porridge, and stew. *Pap* is made from *mealies*, another word for corn. *Morogo* is a combination of different types of green leaves, including beet leaves, which are boiled and served with pap. Meat is popular throughout South Africa. Mopane worms, fried locusts, and dried meat called *biltong* are sometimes eaten as snacks.

Daily life

South Africans love to have *braaie* (barbecues) whenever they can. It is a great social occasion and a way of life for all cultures. Steaks, chops, and spicy sausages called *boerewors* are usually on the menu.

Buttermilk rusks

Ask an adult to help you make these delicious rusks (a type of bread).

Ingredients

- 13 ounces (3 sticks, plus 2 tablespoons) butter
- 2 1/2 cups sugar
- 2 large eggs
- 3 1/3 pounds (12 cups) self-rising flour (sifted)
- 2 tablespoons baking powder
- 2 1/4 cups buttermilk (or use a mixture of milk and natural yogurt)

What to do

1. Preheat the oven to 350 °F (180 °C).
2. Mix the butter and sugar together, and then add the eggs one at a time. Mix in the sifted flour and baking powder. Add the buttermilk and mix with a fork. Knead lightly to make a dough.
3. Place small balls of dough on greased bread pans. Bake in the middle of the oven for 45 to 55 minutes.
4. Separate and place the rusks on a cooling rack. Put them in the cool oven (with the door open) for 4–5 hours or overnight to dry out.

Sports

South Africa has a great history in sports, including two wins in the **rugby** World Cup. In 1995 it won the cup in South Africa. Nelson Mandela was there to celebrate and hugged the captain, Francois Pienaar, a white Afrikaner. It was a moment that demonstrated how far the country had come. This story was told in the 2009 movie *Invictus*. **Cricket** is another team sport that South Africans enjoy, while soccer is also extremely popular, particularly since South Africa hosted the 2010 World Cup. While South Africans enjoy attending sporting events, they also like going to bars to watch them on big screens. Often the atmosphere is almost as exciting as at live matches.

MAKHAYA NTINI
(BORN 1977)

Makhaya Ntini was the first black cricket player to play for South Africa. He was born in Mdingi, in Cape Province. He worked as a cattle herder before playing cricket. Ntini first played for South Africa in 1998 and continued until 2011. He was one of South Africa's most successful players.

South Africans are passionate about sports. This soccer fan has decorated her face with the South African flag.

Water sports

Good weather means that South Africans enjoy trips to the coast and visiting national parks. Golden Mile beach in KwaZulu-Natal is protected by shark nets, so that people can safely swim and surf. Some people go diving and get to see sharks up close.

YOUNG PEOPLE

"Kick it up" was a program that gave 20 South African girls the opportunity to tell their stories about the World Cup. The girls were trained in digital media by sports journalists and sportswomen. The girls then wrote and made their own videos, giving them a voice in a male-dominated world.

South Africa Today

White South Africa has changed since the end of **apartheid**. There are many different communities in South Africa today. Most have only recently had the opportunity to affect South African life. For example, black South Africans did not gain the right to vote until 1994. While South Africa has changed since the end of apartheid, there is still a big gap between the rich and poor. The rich are still mainly white, and the poor are mainly black. This gap is also still large in education. Crime is a big issue, as is **HIV/AIDS**. Attempts to close the gap between **ethnic** groups is proving a slow and difficult process.

However, progress has been made. Most people's lives are better than they had been during the apartheid years. Many more people have homes with running water and electricity. The HIV/AIDS crisis is finally coming under some control, and **life expectancy** is once again rising.

Pride

Many things could have gone wrong in the change from apartheid to **democracy**. Some people thought that civil war, when two or more groups within a country fight each other, might happen. However, the changeover happened fairly peacefully, and most South Africans are proud of that.

Looking forward

In South Africa today, most young people know their history, but understand that things have changed and will continue to do so. There is genuine pride in South Africa, and a hope that theirs will be—even if it is not yet—the most free and open-minded country in the world.

As Nelson Mandela said, "We must regard the healing of the South African nation as a process, not an event." The improvements will take time, and the children of today will one day see the benefit.

Fact File

Name:	**Republic** of South Africa
Capital:	Pretoria (administrative); Cape Town (legislative); Bloemfontein (judicial)
Largest city:	Johannesburg
Language:	11 official languages, including English, Afrikaans, Zulu, and Xhosa
Population:	49,004,031 (July 2011 est.)
Life expectancy at birth:	men—50.1 years; women—48.3 years
Religion:	mainly Christian
Currency:	1 Rand = 100 cents
Area:	471,000 square miles (1.22 million square kilometers)
Bordering countries:	Botswana; Lesotho; Swaziland; Namibia; Zimbabwe; Mozambique (Lesotho and Swaziland lie within S. Africa.)
Lowest point:	Atlantic Ocean, at 0 feet (0 meters)
Highest mountain:	Mafadi, at 11,319 feet (3,450 meters)
Longest river:	Gariep River (also known as the Orange River), at 1,300 miles (2,092 kilometers)
Resources:	gold; diamonds; coal; nickel; platinum; natural gas; salt
Imports:	machinery; chemicals; foods; petroleum products
Exports:	gold; chromium; diamonds; platinum; coal; machinery; wine; citrus fruits such as grapefruit
National anthem:	"National Anthem of South Africa." Adopted in 1994, it is a combination of two different anthems previously used by the white and non-white populations.
National symbols:	giant or king protea (flower); springbok (animal); blue crane (bird)

Famous South Africans

Christiaan Barnard (carried out first human heart transplant); Nadine Gordimer (Nobel Prize-winning author); Miriam Makeba (singer and **human rights activist**); Nelson Mandela (former president of South Africa); Oscar Pistorius (Paralympic athlete); Charlize Theron (actress); Natalie du Toit (Olympic and Paralympic swimmer); Desmond Tutu (cleric and anti-**apartheid** campaigner)

National holidays

January 1	New Year's Day
March 21	Human Rights Day
April 27	Freedom Day
May 1	Workers' Day
June 16	Youth Day
August 9	National Women's Day
September 24	Heritage Day
December 16	Day of Reconciliation
December 25	Christmas Day
December 26	Day of Good Will

Blue cranes are only found in South Africa.

Timeline

BCE means "before the common era." When this appears after a date, it refers to the number of years before the Christian religion began. BCE dates are always counted backward.

CE means "common era." When this appears after a date, it refers to the time after the Christian religion began.

3.4 million–1.4 million years BCE **Fossils** dating to this time show different stages of hominid (early human) development.

200,000–100,000 years BCE Modern humans appear in South Africa.

30,000–20,000 years BCE **Ancestors** of the modern-day San live in South Africa.

about 3rd–8th centuries CE Bantu-speaking people from the north settle alongside the San and Khoikhoi.

about 11th–14th centuries CE Iron Age kingdoms appear in the northeastern corner of South Africa. Trade networks begin to appear.

1652	Jan van Riebeeck founds the Cape Colony, on behalf of the Dutch East India Company.
1806	The British seize the Cape Colony from the Dutch.
mid-1830s	**Boers** make the Great Trek north to escape British rule.
1867	Diamonds are discovered near Kimberley.
1879	The Anglo-Zulu War begins. The British defeat the Zulus in Natal.
1880–81	The first Anglo-Boer War is fought, which eventually ends with peace and the Transvaal restored as a **republic**.
1886	Gold is found near what is now Johannesburg.
1887	The British conquer Zululand.
1899–1902	The second Boer War is fought.
1910	The Union of South Africa is created.
1912	The South African Native National Congress is formed. It is now better known as the ANC.

1913	The Natives Land Act is passed, to keep most land in the hands of white people.
1950	The National Party sets up **apartheid** measures after winning elections.
1952	Pass Laws come into effect, meaning non-whites need to carry identity papers at all times.
1960	The Sharpeville Massacre occurs; the ANC is banned.
1961	South Africa becomes a republic and leaves the British **Commonwealth**.
1964	Nelson Mandela is imprisoned.
1976	Student protestors in Soweto are shot at by police, leading to riots and the death of hundreds of people.
1977	Steve Biko is killed while in police **custody**.
1986	**Economic sanctions** are placed on South Africa.
1990	Nelson Mandela is released from prison, and bans on the ANC and other groups are lifted.
1993	Discussions to formally end apartheid are completed.
1994	Mandela wins the first **democratic** elections (as part of the ANC) and becomes the first black president of South Africa. South Africa becomes part of the Commonwealth once more.
1995	The Truth and Reconciliation Commission, headed by Archbishop Desmond Tutu, is set up to investigate apartheid crimes.
1999	Mandela steps down as president, but the ANC wins again and Thabo Mbeki becomes president.
2003	The government promises **HIV/AIDS** drugs that had previously been banned because they were too expensive.
2007	Helen Zille is made leader of the Democratic Alliance, a major political party.
2009	The ANC win a fourth election, and Jacob Zuma becomes president. South Africa officially enters a **recession**.
2010	Soccer's World Cup is held in South Africa.

Glossary

ancestor person from the past that someone is descended from

apartheid legalized system of keeping people of different races separate, which was in place between 1950 and 1993 in South Africa

assimilation way in which a minority is brought under the control of a ruling power, by gradually taking up their beliefs and traditions

Boer South African of Dutch descent

colonial relating to a colony; a country that is ruled by another country

Commonwealth organization made up of countries that used to be part of the British Empire

concentration camp place in which large numbers of people, often minorities such as Jews in World War II, are imprisoned. The camps are usually crowded and have very basic facilities.

conservation caring for the environment and protecting rare species of animals and plants

cricket bat and ball game played on an oval field; it is similar to baseball

custody place, usually prison, where people are kept by police

democracy political system in which the government is made up of members who have been chosen by the people of the country

democratic relating to a democracy

economic sanctions ban on trading with a particular country

economy relating to money and the industry and jobs in a country

ecosystem living things in their own environment

ethnic classification of people by their race

export goods sold to another country

extinction dying out

faith healing using faith and strong beliefs to heal people who are sick

fossil remains of an ancient animal or plant, found in rock

G8 (Group of Eight) group that includes the world's eight wealthiest countries, who meet regularly to discuss economic and political issues

HIV/AIDS virus and disease that attacks the body's defenses. Sufferers are then more likely to become sick from other diseases.

human rights activist person who works to protect or promote human rights, such as the right to food and shelter and to speak freely

hunter-gatherer person who lives mainly by hunting and fishing, and by harvesting wild food

hydroelectric power electricity made by flowing water

import good or resource brought into a country

investment act of putting money into a company or project, often with the aim to make money

life expectancy how long people live on average in an area

mixed ancestry person who has parents of different racial backgrounds

parliament ruling body of some countries; laws are made there

recession slowing down of the economy over a period of time

renewable energy energy that will not run out, such as that created by the sun or wind

republic country in which the head of state is not a king or queen but rather a president. Citizens can vote for the people they want to represent them in the government.

resource means available for a country to develop, such as minerals and energy sources

rugby ball game played with an oval ball that can be kicked, thrown, or passed; it is similar to football

rural relating to the countryside

solar relating to the sun

species type of animal or plant

township town on the edge of a city that was home to non-white South Africans during the apartheid years. Townships still exist, and many poor, often black, South Africans still live in them. But people are no longer forced to stay there legally.

wetlands land of swamps or marshes

Find Out More

Books

Brown, Laaren, and Lenny Hort. *Nelson Mandela* (*DK Biography*). New York: Dorling Kindersley, 2006.

Clark, Domini. *South Africa: The People* (*Lands, Peoples, and Cultures*). New York: Crabtree, 2009.

Gallagher, Michael. *South Africa* (*Countries in the News*). North Mankato, Minn.: Smart Apple Media, 2008.

Green, Jen. *Focus on South Africa* (*World in Focus*). Milwaukee: World Almanac Library, 2007.

Koosmann, Melissa. *The Fall of Apartheid* (*Monumental Milestones*). Hockessin, Del.: Mitchell Lane, 2009.

Senker, Cath. *South Africa* (*Letters from Around the World*). North Mankato, Minn.: Cherrytree, 2005.

Websites

http://kids.nationalgeographic.com/kids/places/find/south-africa/
This site has lots of facts about South Africa, as well as a link to pictures of South African wildlife.

www.timeforkids.com/TFK/kids/hh/goplaces/ article/0,28376,590849,00.html
Find out more about South Africa and learn how to speak a few Zulu phrases!

www.timeforkids.com/TFK/specials/goplaces/0,12405,384367,00.html
Read an interview with Nelson Mandela in which he talks about children in South Africa.

Places to visit

If you ever get the chance to go to South Africa, here are some of the places you could visit:

The Apartheid Museum in Johannesburg

www.apartheidmuseum.org

If you want to learn more about **apartheid**, then this is the place to go. There are exhibits that explain why apartheid happened and what life was like under it.

Soweto

www.joburg.org.za/Soweto

The famous township of Soweto is an interesting place to visit. It is best to take a guided tour.

Kimberley Mine Museum and "Big Hole"

www.thebighole.co.za

If you are interested in diamond mining, visit Kimberley to learn more at the open-air museum there. You can even tour the mines themselves.

Robben Island

www.robben-island.org.za

While now a museum and tourist attraction, for many years Robben Island was a prison. Nelson Mandela was held there.

Hluhluwe-Imfolozi Game Reserve

www.southafrica-travel.net/Parks/e_umfolo.htm

This park in Zululand is one of the oldest game reserves in South Africa. You can see the "Big Five" animals here.

Table Mountain National Park

www.sanparks.org/parks/table_mountain/

This national park includes one of the most famous of South Africa's landmarks, Table Mountain, as well as the Cape of Good Hope.

Topic Tools

You can use these topic tools for your school projects. Trace the map onto a sheet of paper, using the thick black outline to guide you.

The South African flag has existed since 1994. It has red, white, and blue parts that are from the British and Dutch flags. The other colors—green, gold, and black—are those of the ANC. The Y shape represents all the South African people moving forward together. Copy the flag design and then color in your picture. Make sure you use the right colors!

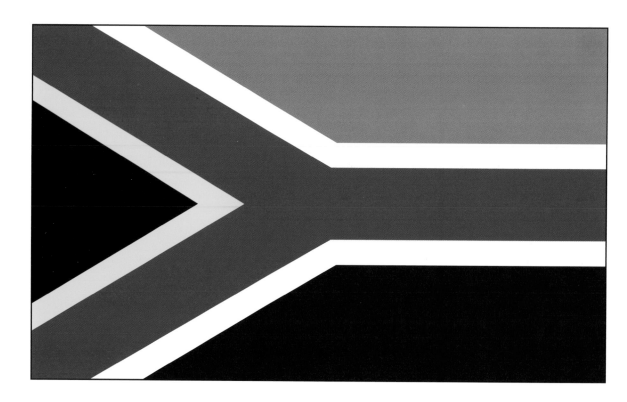

N

■ Pretoria

■ Bloemfontein

■ Cape Towm

Index

Titles in the series

Afghanistan	978 1 4329 5195 5	Japan	978 1 4329 6102 2
Algeria	978 1 4329 6093 3	Latvia	978 1 4329 5211 2
Australia	978 1 4329 6094 0	Liberia	978 1 4329 6103 9
Brazil	978 1 4329 5196 2	Libya	978 1 4329 6104 6
Canada	978 1 4329 6095 7	Lithuania	978 1 4329 5212 9
Chile	978 1 4329 5197 9	Mexico	978 1 4329 5213 6
China	978 1 4329 6096 4	Morocco	978 1 4329 6105 3
Costa Rica	978 1 4329 5198 6	New Zealand	978 1 4329 6106 0
Cuba	978 1 4329 5199 3	North Korea	978 1 4329 6107 7
Czech Republic	978 1 4329 5200 6	Pakistan	978 1 4329 5214 3
Egypt	978 1 4329 6097 1	Philippines	978 1 4329 6108 4
England	978 1 4329 5201 3	Poland	978 1 4329 5215 0
Estonia	978 1 4329 5202 0	Portugal	978 1 4329 6109 1
France	978 1 4329 5203 7	Russia	978 1 4329 6110 7
Germany	978 1 4329 5204 4	Scotland	978 1 4329 5216 7
Greece	978 1 4329 6098 8	South Africa	978 1 4329 6112 1
Haiti	978 1 4329 5205 1	South Korea	978 1 4329 6113 8
Hungary	978 1 4329 5206 8	Spain	978 1 4329 6111 4
Iceland	978 1 4329 6099 5	Tunisia	978 1 4329 6114 5
India	978 1 4329 5207 5	United States of America	978 1 4329 6115 2
Iran	978 1 4329 5208 2	Vietnam	978 1 4329 6116 9
Iraq	978 1 4329 5209 9	Wales	978 1 4329 5217 4
Ireland	978 1 4329 6100 8	Yemen	978 1 4329 5218 1
Israel	978 1 4329 6101 5		
Italy	978 1 4329 5210 5		